WORD PLAY SERIES

HOME SWEET HOME

Acompanhe o relato de Homer, uma ave muito especial com uma singular maneira de enxergar a própria vida. Sem perceber, você se envolverá na história, seguindo as pistas dadas pelo texto e pelas ilustrações. E verá que mais do que nos contar sobre sua natureza, seus hábitos e suas aventuras, Homer nos faz refletir sobre a *nossa* natureza, imperfeitos seres humanos.

editora ática

My name is Homer. That is the name of a famous poet from ancient Greece. But I am not a poet, oh no! And I am not human. I am a bird. You can see me clearly in the picture. I am not a chicken. I am not a duck. I am a pigeon. A beautiful gray pigeon. I am not in the tree. I am not on the ground. I am on the roof of the little house.

Can you find Homer in the picture? Is he on the left, in the middle, or on the right side of the picture?
Can you also find a chicken and a duck? Where are they?

This is Mr. Goodman, my owner. I live in the garden of his house, in the suburbs of a big city. Mr. Goodman is not very popular around here. People say he is not very honest, sometimes they call him Mr. Badman. I don't know. I don't understand human nature. I like him. He is good to me and to my brothers and sisters. He gives us food and water, he gives us a home — that's all we need. We find safety and protection here, especially in the winter. It's good to be home when it's raining or snowing. It's very cold now. We are all in the little house. Mr. Goodman is feeding my brothers and sisters. They all like corn, but I don't.

What part of the year is it in the picture?
Who are Homer's brothers and sisters?
Why are all the pigeons in the little house?
Can you find Homer in the picture? Is he on the left, in the middle, or on the right side of the picture?

Today is Sunday, a great day. It's early morning now, the sun is rising. A beautiful sunrise. It's not cold and the sky is clear. A perfect day to spend outdoors, in the open air. We are all going out in a few minutes. Mr. Goodman is taking us to a park in his old station-wagon. My cage is in the car, between number eleven and number eight. Mr. Goodman is near the car, but he can't find his keys.

Can you find Homer among his brothers and sisters? What number is his cage?
Mr. Goodman does not know where his car keys are. Can you help him find them? Where are they?
The sky is a very light pink color. Can you say why?

2
4
7
8
11
6
3
10
9
5

Mr. Goodman has a powerful voice. In his exotic green clothes he attracts a lot of people, especially children. He is shouting something about Ecology. I don't know exactly what it is, because I don't understand the human language very well. He uses the word *liberty*. Is it another word for freedom?

Many people come and stay around us. They all look like friends, but wait a moment... I can see an enemy in front of my cage now.

Why is Mr. Goodman wearing green clothes?
Can you find Homer in the picture? Who is in front of his cage?

HOME SWEET HOME

WORD PLAY SERIES

EXPLORING WORDS AND IDEAS

YES OR NO?

1 **Assinale *Yes* ou *No*, de acordo com a correção de cada frase em relação ao texto.**

		Yes	*No*
(page 2)	Homer is the name of a famous poet from modern Greece.		
(page 2)	Homer, the bird in the story, is a white pigeon.		
(page 4)	Mr. Goodman has a lot of pigeons in his garden.		
(page 4)	Mr. Goodman lives outside the city center.		
(page 4)	Homer's brothers and sisters are the other pigeons.		
(page 6)	Mr. Goodman's pigeons fly to the park.		
(page 8)	Mr. Goodman uses the word *liberty*, another word for *freedom*.		
(page 8)	Cats and pigeons are friends, not enemies.		
(page 12)	Mr. Goodman's birds enjoy freedom just for a short time.		
(page 14)	The instinct of a homing pigeon is to fly back home.		

WHERE IS EVERYTHING?

2 **Você se lembra onde, nesta história, estão desenhadas as coisas abaixo? Volte a olhar as ilustrações e assinale as páginas onde primeiro elas aparecem.**

page ☐ an apple

page ☐ a cat

page ☐ a beautiful sunrise

page ☐ two keys

page ☐ a chicken

page ☐ some black clouds

page ☐ a duck

page ☐ an old lady

page ☐ a station-wagon

page ☐ a green hat

page ☐ a little girl

page ☐ a tree

SAY IT IN ENGLISH

3 **Observe o modelo desta frase:**

After — **(*depois de* — preposição)**

flying freely for some miles... — **(*voar* — forma verbal em *ing*)**

Siga o modelo passando as frases abaixo para o inglês.

a Depois de alimentar os pássaros... (*to feed*)

____

b Depois de segurar o pombo por um momento... (*to hold*)

____

c Depois de dar o dinheiro para Mr. Goodman... (*to give*)

____

O mesmo se aplica a outras preposições, como *before* (antes de), *for* (para), etc. Refaça as frases acima, substituindo *after* por *before* ou *for*.

HOMER'S NATURE

4 **Combine as colunas, fazendo associações dos substantivos, de acordo com a natureza do personagem principal da história, Homer the pigeon.**

a A cat	( ) More powerful than liberty.
b Winter	( ) Friends.
c Mr. Goodman's garden	( ) Important, but not necessary.
d The sun	( ) Safety and protection.
e Corn	( ) An enemy.
f Children	( ) A guide.
g Homing instinct	( ) Time to stay at home.
h Mr. Goodman	( ) Good food.
i Liberty	( ) A friend.
j An apple	( ) Good food for pigeons, but not for Homer.

BETWEEN OR AMONG?

5 **Escolha entre *between* (entre — dois elementos) e *among* (entre — vários elementos) para completar cada uma das frases a seguir.**

a) Can you find Homer ________________ his brothers and sisters?

b) ________________ the people around the cages there is an old lady with a cat.

c) Homer's cage is ________________ number eleven and number eight.

d) Corn is not ________________ Homer's favorite foods.

e) Homer can always find the way ________________ the park and Mr. Goodman's garden.

WHAT'S THE MESSAGE?

6 **Identifique cada uma das ações ilustradas, escrevendo as respectivas letras na coluna vertical, de modo a formar uma mensagem.**

An old lady is feeding some birds. ☐
A teacher is telling a story. ☐
A woman is taking the children to school. ☐
A man is shouting for help. ☐
The sun is rising. ☐

A woman is wearing strange clothes. ☐
A cat is sitting on the roof. ☐

A boy is waiting for his girlfriend. ☐
A bird is flying in the sky. ☐
A duck is drinking water. ☐
A child is playing with some keys. ☐

GIVE THE OPPOSITES

7 Complete as frases com os opostos das palavras em destaque.

a (page 2) Homer is the name of a famous poet from ________ Greece, not from modern Greece.

b (page 4) Mr. Goodman is ________ to the pigeons; he is not bad to them.

c (page 8) A pigeon sees a cat not as a friend, but as an ________.

d (page 10) The child's father ________ Mr. Goodman some money. Mr. Goodman takes the money.

e (page 10) In a moment Homer is going to be not ____ the cage, but out of it.

f (page 12) There are a lot of dark clouds in the sky now. It is cloudy. It is not ________ now.

g (page 14) Mr. Goodman takes the pigeons to a different park every Sunday and their instinct ________ them back.

h (page 14) They can ________ find their home. They never have trouble finding it.

ANSWER THE QUESTIONS

8 **Responda em inglês, observando o número da página que aparece entre parênteses.**

1 (page 2) Where is Homer?

2 (page 4) What is Mr. Goodman doing?

3 (page 6) Where are the pigeons going on that Sunday morning?

4 (page 8) What can Homer see in front of his cage?

5 (page 10) What is the child's father giving Mr. Goodman?

6 (page 12) Why can't Homer see the sun now?

7 (page 14) Why is it easy for those birds to find their way home?

MATCH THE COLUMNS

9 **Combine as colunas encontrando a resposta adequada a cada pergunta.**

1 When?	a Mr. Goodman.
2 Where?	b As a guide for my sense of direction.
3 What?	c In a few minutes.
4 Why?	d All.
5 How?	e In the suburbs of a big city.
6 Who?	f Some money, the price of my freedom.
7 How much?	g An apple, my favorite food.
8 How many?	h Because there are a lot of dark clouds in the sky.

COMPLETE THE SENTENCES

10 **Escolha cada um dos verbos entre parênteses de modo a completar corretamente as frases.**

1 I am ____________ through the air. (holding/flying)

2 It's early morning now, the sun is ____________. (rising/living)

3 Mr. Goodman is in the park, ____________ something about ecology. (spending/shouting)

4 Homer is ____________ on an apple, his favorite food. (feeling/feeding)

5 Mr. Goodman is ____________ the birds to a park in his old station-wagon. (finding/taking)

6 It's good to be home when it's raining or ____________. (trying/snowing)

7 They are all ____________ in a few minutes. (going out/wearing)

8 The man is ____________ the birds food and water. (giving/staying)

DO YOU REMEMBER?

Você é capaz de reproduzir, de memória, no balão abaixo, o que o Mr. Goodman está gritando, no parque? (pág. 9)

Liberty for the birds!
ECOLOGY NEEDS YOU

This is exciting. In a moment I am going to be out of the cage, in the hands of a child. The child's father gives Mr. Goodman some money, the price of my freedom. The little girl is going to hold me in her nervous hands for a moment. Then she is going to let me go. Some of my brothers and sisters are free already. I am next!

Mr. Goodman has a strange business. What does he sell?
What is the price of Homer's freedom?
How many of Homer's brothers and sisters (pigeons only) are free already?
Can you find Homer in the picture? Who is in front of his cage now?

ECOLOGY NEEDS YOU
4
3
1
9
10
12

Freedom! I am flying through the air once more. It's good to be free again. It's good to enjoy complete freedom but ... I am trying to find my way home.

The sky is not clear now. There are a lot of dark clouds, and I can't see the sun. I use the sun as a guide for my sense of direction. The position of the sun helps me fly in a certain direction. And nature tells me to fly home now. Can you help me find it?

Can you help Homer find the sun in the picture? Is it on the left, in the middle, or on the right side?
Can you see something strange in the clouds? What is it?

Home sweet home! After flying freely for some miles I am home again. I am now on the ground, feeding on an apple, my favorite food. My instinct and my sense of direction bring me back. That happens every Sunday. Mr. Goodman takes us to a different park every Sunday, sometimes a park in another town or city. Sometimes it's very far from home, but there is no trouble for me or the other pigeons. We can always find our way home. We are homing pigeons, or homers. That's my name, remember?

Why does Homer return to Mr. Goodman's garden?
Why is Goodman an ironic name in the story?
Can you find Homer in this picture? Where is he? What is he doing?

A LITTLE HELP

air: ar
already: já
always: sempre
among: entre (vários)
ancient: antigo
around: em volta (de)
as: como
to attract: atrair
back: de volta
beautiful: belo
between: entre (dois)
bicycle: bicicleta
bird: pássaro, ave
to bring: trazer
business: negócio
cage: gaiola
to call: chamar
chicken: frango; galinha
child/children: criança/crianças
clear: claro; limpo, sem nuvens
clothes: roupa(s)
cloud: nuvem
cloudy: nublado
cold: frio
to come: vir

corn: milho
dark: escuro
direction: direção
duck: pato
early: cedo
enemy: inimigo
to enjoy: gozar, desfrutar (de)
exciting: emocionante
far (from): longe (de)
to feed: alimentar
to feed on: alimentar-se de
few: poucos
a few: alguns
to find: achar, encontrar
to fly: voar

food: comida, alimento
free: livre
freedom: liberdade
garden: jardim
to give: dar
to go out: sair
gray: cinzento
great: grande
Greece: Grécia
ground: chão
guide: guia
hand: mão
to happen: acontecer
hat: chapéu
here: aqui
to hold: segurar

homer (= homing pigeon): pombo-correio
Homer: Homero
human: humano
instinct: instinto
ironic: irônico
key: chave
language: língua
left: esquerdo, esquerda
to let: deixar, permitir
liberty: liberdade
light: claro; luz
to look like: parecer
middle: meio, centro
mile: milha
more: mais
nature: natureza
to need: precisar (de)
next: próximo
once: uma vez
outdoors: fora de casa
owner: dono
pigeon: pombo
pink: cor-de-rosa
powerful: poderoso

price: preço
protection: proteção
to rain: chover
to remember: lembrar(-se) (de)
to return: retornar
right: direito, direita
to rise: (sol) nascer
roof: telhado
safety: segurança
to say: dizer
to see: ver
to sell: vender
sense: sentido, senso
to shout: gritar
side: lado
sky: céu
to snow: nevar
to spend: passar (tempo)
station-wagon: camioneta, perua
to stay: ficar, permanecer
strange: estranho
sun: sol
Sunday: domingo
sunrise: nascer do sol
sweet: doce
to take: levar; tomar
to tell: contar, dizer a
then: então
through: através (de)

tree: árvore
trouble: problema, dificuldade
to try: tentar
to understand: entender
voice: voz
to wait: esperar
way: caminho; modo
to wear: usar, vestir
well: bem
winter: inverno
word: palavra